A THREAD OF BELONGING

CLAIRE ELIZABETH GROSE

Copyright © 2021 by Claire Elizabeth Grose

Compiled and edited by Michael Grose and June Kennedy

All rights reserved. No portion of this publication may be reproduced, stored in a retrieval system or transmitted in any form by any means – electronic, mechanical, photocopying, recording, or any other –except for brief quotation in printed reviews, without the prior written permission of the publisher.

Unless indicated otherwise, all scripture quotations in this book are from the following source:

The Good News Bible: The Bible in Today's English Version (TEV) © 1976 by the American Bible Society. Used with permission.

ISBN 978-0-6486884-5-7

Author contact information - clairegrose.heartmatters@gmail.com

Version 1.0

DEDICATION

This book is dedicated to June and Hugh
My beloved sister and brother-in-law

CONTENTS

DEDICATION .... **IV**

CONTENTS .... **V**

PREFACE .... **VIII**

ACKNOWLEDGEMENTS .... **X**

    PART ONE 1
        MY DAILY PRAYER 4
        ENCOUNTER GOD 5
        CORDS OF LIGHT 6
        MORNING PRAYERS 7
        HEALING BALM 8
        NATURE'S GALLERY 9
        HEART MATTERS 10
        TOUCHED BY A RAINBOW 11
        TODAY'S TASK 14
        INSIDE OUT 15
        TIMES OF CHANGE 16
        DUSK ON SHOW 17
        OUR RELATIONSHIP BLOSSOMS 18
        PURE LOVE 19
        IN WANT I COME TO YOU 20
        FOREVER LOVE 21
        ELEMENTS IN TIME 22
        JESUS LOVES THE WORLD 23
        EXPECT TO RECEIVE 26
        SEASONS OF LIFE 27
        LEAD ME IN YOUR FOOTSTEPS 28
        CLAIM A HAPPY DAY 29
    PART TWO 30
        A THREAD OF BELONGING 33
        IN PERFECT COMMUNION 34
        SILENT LISTENER, UNSEEN GUEST 35
        YOUR HEART CAN BE HIS HOME 36

THE TEST OF TIME	37
THE NEXT TWENTY FOUR HOURS	38
THE HUMAN HEART	41
SHARE TODAY	42
OUR WATCHFUL SHEPHERD	43
STEP OUT IN HIS LIGHT	44
SOLID GROUND	45
ONE TO ONE	46
YOUR HOPE HE WILL RESTORE	49
MY POEMS	50
MY MIND'S EYE	51
FORGET REGRET	52
MY HEART YOU OWN	53
THE BEST IS YET TO COME	54
MAKE HIM YOUR GOAL	57
MAKE A FRESH START	58
KEEP ME ON TRACK	59
HEAL ME LORD	60
IN HIS SHADOW	61
AN OPEN HEART	62
HE'S BY YOUR SIDE	63
GIFTS HE LONGS TO GIVE	64
DIRECTION	65
COMMIT THE DAY	66
LIFE'S QUALITIES	67
YOUR NEEDS WILL BE MET	68
PART THREE	69
THE VOICE IN ME	72
YOU TURNED MY LIFE AROUND	73
TODAY WE HAVE JESUS	74
PRIVILEGED POWERS	75
PURE GOLD	76
RUNAWAY TEARS	77
SWEET VICTORY	80
WHERE AM I	81

ETERNAL SPRING	*82*
OVERFLOWING HOLINESS	*83*
WALK IN UNISON WITH CHRIST	*84*
PRECIOUS GIFTS	*85*
PART FOUR	86
FOLLOW YOUR HEART TO THE CROSS	*89*
YOUR GREATEST BLESSING IN A VOW	*90*
GOD'S HOLY PLAN	*91*
A BRAND NEW LOVE	*94*
FOLLOW HIS PATH	*95*
A JOURNEY LIKE NO OTHER	*98*
A GIFT BEYOND COMPARE	*99*
UNSPOKEN LOVE	*100*
FAITHFUL SERVANTS	*101*

PREFACE

Two things I just wanted to say about this book are, why I started writing and how I came by the title.

I grew up in the 1950's-1960's in Adelaide, South Australia, my life was pretty simple but wonderful. I was very lucky to have a secure family life, and my Mum and Dad brought the family up to treat others with respect, do the right thing, be courteous, and respect your elders. We had a strict upbringing and even as adults our parents never criticized us but encouraged us to do our best in life. They were "Aussie battlers" but we always managed to make it through the tough times!

They were people of integrity and cared about others and instilled that into our family.

Church was a big part of our lives growing up. We went to Sunday School at an early age and progressed up through the appropriate groups as we got older.

Youth groups, camps and church anniversaries were all important to the whole family. We competed in church sports teams, basketball and tennis with other parishes across Adelaide. Life-long friendships were in the making and cherished golden memories to look back on that would never fade.

Bible stories, hymns and choruses were all part of getting to know Jesus. This nurturing finally led me to the day Jesus came knocking on my heart's door. Being filled with the Holy Spirit is something I will never forget and the overwhelming power of His love that filled my whole being and propelled me to the front of the hall to give my heart to Him. No words can fully describe the joy I felt. That was in February 1968, I was 14 years of age. He has been my Shining Light ever since, and lives within me always.

So I thank my beautiful Mum and Dad for the way they raised me and for the foundation of knowing Jesus' love.

It was in His love that I started to write, in the autumn of 1993. My journey has brought me to this book "A Thread of Belonging", which is all you need for God to do His work in your heart through the Holy Spirit! He can turn your belonging into a great magnitude that will transform your life!

"...I assure you that if you have faith as big as a mustard seed,.... you could do anything!" (Matthew 17:20) Good News Bible.

The title came to me simply by looking at my own journey from a child until now, and how He truly has turned my life around by maintaining my trust and faith in Him no matter what life threw at me.

When I was a young Christian reading my Bible was really important to me in getting to know Jesus as my personal Saviour and became the foundation that I built my faith on.

It gave me strength and courage as I began life in the workforce at the age of 16. Coming from a sheltered upbringing it was my lifeline to self-confidence and adapting to social life at work.
The poems reflect the everyday feelings and emotions that we feel as we meet the challenges of life and how the great magnitude of God's love can help us rise above them.

I pray you will seek His eternal counsel in your everyday life and receive His grace and mercy in "A Thread of Belonging".

Many of these writings have been my first words of whispered prayer, so much that I have been moved to write them down at once and continue on in His wonderful and absolute love.

Together we write as He provides my inspiration.

All glory to Him, my precious Lord Jesus!

ACKNOWLEDGEMENTS

My heartfelt thanks to my beloved family, my Mum and Dad, Lilly and Ken, and my siblings Jeanette, June, Carol, Gloria and Lynne, for their never ending encouragement and support to me. To the rest of the family, you are all a precious link that joins us together.

To Michael and Andrew for your continual support to me in fulfilling my passion of writing poems for the Lord to help others through His Word.

A huge thank you to Junie for editing my poems and the coffees and lunches we enjoyed along the way.

To Joy Furnell for her Crown of Thorns drawing, you have an amazing gift, thank you Joy.

Special thanks to Hugh for the glorious snow cover photo taken on the banks of the River Clyde, Lanark, Scotland.

A big thank you to Lynne, Eileen and Val for photos also.

To my friends and Church Families, thank you for your love and support.

To my beautiful sons, Michael and Andrew, thank you for loving me, and I am so glad He gave you to me. I will love you forever. To your Partners and my Grandchildren I love you all so much.

To you the reader, thank you for picking this book up and I pray you will find His peace and love on the pages ahead.

May He shower you all with His love and blessings.

PART ONE

"I assure you that if you have faith as
big as a mustard seed…..You could do anything!"

Matthew 17 : 20

A THREAD OF BELONGING

IN TRUST…
WATCH YOUR FAITH GROW…

"For it is by our faith that we are
put right with God; …"

Romans 10 : 10

MY DAILY PRAYER

Be with me, stay with me,
Close by my side,
Fill me with Your peace and love,
So my spirit shall surely fly
To the heights in Your love,
As only You can give,
Prepare me for this day ahead,
So in me You'll always live.

ENCOUNTER GOD

Encounter God,
Bring your thoughts to rest,
Be still in His presence,
The silent, unseen guest!

Encounter God,
In the hush of day
Listen for His voice,
He longs for you today.

Wait at His Throne,
Share your deepest care,
He's thrilled with your victory
Because a kind word you shared.

Encounter God,
Make your life worthwhile,
His sacrifice made you special,
Will you go the extra mile?

Encounter God,
Learn His ways and Words,
An awakening of His power
Because your heart His Spirit stirred!

CORDS OF LIGHT

A union of love so strong
Bound with cords of light,
Beamed from heaven's shore
Will hold you so tight.

Cords of light from heaven,
A wonder in many ways,
From the Saviour so pure
Can be yours today.

Cords of light are beams
Straight to your heart and soul,
Channels for His love
Through His Spirit can unfold.

His cords of light will hold you
For the length of time,
You only have to ask Him,
"Jesus be mine."

A union of love between you
Held by the cords of light
Will never be broken,
You are precious in His sight.

MORNING PRAYERS

Morning prayers so special
While dawn is waking up,
All is fresh and new,
My mind is clear enough.

I thank You for another day
And say "I love You so",
"Give me strength for the hours ahead
While I walk today's road."

In morning prayers I rest in Thee,
There's quiet all around,
Evidence of damp and mist
Moving to higher ground.

My morning prayers are the best,
In silence I wait for Thee,
Just to be in Your presence Lord,
Is good enough for me.

HEALING BALM

A healing balm so pure
From the Saviour above,
Is ours for the taking
When we know His love.

You can find it in a sunset
Or ripples to the shore,
A bird taking flight
Or a mountain and waterfall.

As soothing as a breeze
On a summer's night,
Or watching the rain through a window
Makes the heart feel right.

A full moon and stars
Fill the sky at night,
His glorious wonder
For you and I.

Take hold of His healing balm
For peace within,
Nurture your soul
With the King of Kings.

NATURE'S GALLERY

In want I see Your creation
And marvel at Your works,
Your formation and colours,
On this precious earth.

In the world around me
I see You brilliantly,
Its gardens, forests and waterfalls
Brings You close to me.

Your seasons have their purpose,
Misty rain brings peace surreal,
While spring and summer sunshine
Beckon growth for harvest yields.

So thank You dear Lord
For nature's gallery,
Her constant changing scenes
Always bring wonder to me.

HEART MATTERS

Ask the Lord for His loving care
When heart matters rule the day,
Place them in His hands,
Then go on your way.

He has your best interest at heart,
There's nothing He'd rather do,
Relax and enjoy your day,
He will help you see it through.

No matter how slight or complex
These heart matters become,
Give them all to the Saviour
In His time the answer will come.

Your heart matters are in His hands
He knows each one well,
You only have to ask Him,
He is by your side to help.

So refresh your heart matters today
With trust and faith in your soul,
His pierced hands will soothe them
Like the ancient days of old.

TOUCHED BY A RAINBOW

On a showery day
Misty rain drifts in,
Far in the distance
A rainbow begins.

Touching the horizon
And stretching up high,
Lost in the clouds
It appears the other side.

Dampness is all around
But the sun wants to shine,
Peeping through the clouds
As the rainbow stretches high.

So powerful its colours,
Proudly it shows them off,
Being touched by a rainbow
Is joy you cannot stop!

HE CARES FOR EVERYONE...

"I love those who love me;
whoever looks for me can find me."

Proverbs 8 : 17

TODAY'S TASK

The morning is fresh and new,
Scarlet sunrise comes to life,
Morning dew is damp
What a beautiful sight.

Peace calm exist
While life is waking up,
But the day keeps on moving
While I manage today's task.

In every walk of life
Whether it's slow or fast,
Lord help me deal
With today's task.

I may be young or old,
Across the world so wide,
Lord help me with today's task
While I walk today's mile.

INSIDE OUT

Commune with the Saviour
Because He knows your fears and doubts,
There's nothing you can hide,
He knows you inside out.

Stay in touch with the Saviour
To keep your life on track,
Temptations come and go,
Look to Him, don't look back.

Talk with the Saviour
Tell Him your daily needs,
From one dawn to the next
He will help you to succeed.

Commune with Christ, the Lord,
You will want to shout!
Accept Him as your Saviour,
He knows you inside out.

TIMES OF CHANGE

"Where do You want me Lord?"
I have to say,
In these times of change
I have to pray.

You seem closer than ever,
My shield and my guide,
I know You'll always be
Close by my side.

I know You live in Heaven
And You see the times of change,
Let us still remember,
You are still the same.

Yes in these times of change Lord,
Help us to retain
Your sacred love and grace
Because You will never change.

DUSK ON SHOW

Beams of gold stretch to the earth
Streaming behind tall peaks,
Dampness all around
As sunset settles in.

I feel God's presence near
As He marks the end of day,
Take time to view
As He sets the stars in place.

Dusk on show,
Perfect in every way,
May it speak to each heart
Who shares this time of day.

OUR RELATIONSHIP BLOSSOMS

Times alone with You Lord
Are the best for me,
Our relationship blossoms
When I confess my cares to Thee.

Held by Your hands,
How precious they are,
They made the universe
And the evening stars.

Our relationship blossoms
When I make time for Thee,
Your sweetness flows silently
From Your Spirit to me.

Our relationship blossoms
Like blooms on the vine,
In your precious love Lord,
Peace will be mine.

PURE LOVE

Pure love Your sunrise
Triumphant in the sky,
Heralding the day
On her journey way up high.

Pure love your sunset
Bowing to end of day,
Skimming tops of clouds
As she continues on her way.

Pure is Your love,
The almighty King of Kings,
Lover of my soul,
Eternal life You bring.

In awe and in wonder
Your pure love displayed,
In mother nature around us
Where we see You every day.

Pure love the Saviour,
Hallowed You'll always be,
The omnipotent Lord of Lords
Brings me to my knees.

IN WANT I COME TO YOU

In want I come to You Lord,
It's break of day,
A shadow of light appears,
I hear a serenade.

I feel Your love close,
Dawn meets me cool and fresh,
I wake to chirping sounds,
Time of day I love the best.

I give my heart to You,
My greatest need I tell,
In want I come to you,
My fears You will dispel.

So though my needs are great,
Your forgiveness I seek,
In want I come to You,
As we daily meet!

FOREVER LOVE

The precious gift from You Lord
Is Your forever love,
It's beyond our understanding,
It comes from You above.

Your forever love so sacred
Comes with anointing balm,
A symbol of Your Spirit
That cleanses every heart.

Your forever love is supreme
Over every earthly thing,
Nothing can compare
To a love from Eternity.

Forever love so pure,
Divine in every way,
Precious Holy Father
Be mine this very day!

ELEMENTS IN TIME

Summer, Autumn, Winter and Spring,
Bring their elements in time,
Just like our lives,
We weather the changing times.

Some days we wake to sunshine,
All is happy in our world,
Then the leaves begin to fall,
Winter chill comes to call.

But staying strong in the Saviour's love,
A shield that has no end,
Brings the awakening of Spring,
Then the wounds of life will mend

Elements in time are like
Reflections of our moods,
We can stay healthy and strong
In His Word, to help us through.

JESUS LOVES THE WORLD

Pray for His strength,
It's yours to take and share
On the days when light is dim,
Jesus will be there.

He's waiting at your next breath,
He loves you endlessly
To save you from your struggles,
If you ask "Lord, come to me".

His light will never dim,
He will shine eternally,
The light of the world,
In Him you are set free.

His loving arms are waiting
To caress you tenderly,
He says "I love you still,
Beloved come to me".

LIVE IN ME LORD…

"…I live by faith in the Son of God,
who loved me and gave His life for me."

Galatians 2 : 20

EXPECT TO RECEIVE

I focus on Your holiness,
Lowly I bend and kneel
Before Your Throne of gold,
Reverence is what I feel.

I'm quiet now before You
In peace I whisper a prayer,
My cares come to the surface
Which I now share.

The contents of my heart
I can't carry alone,
But I know with You Lord,
I can bring them home.

You are my King of Kings,
Divine healer of heart and soul,
You know all the answers,
Please make me whole.

I need You in my life
To bring comfort and peace,
You are the great healer,
I can expect to receive.

SEASONS OF LIFE

Seasons of life keep changing
The moment we are born,
From that first breath we take
To seeing our every dawn.

Through our growing years
We should reach for the sky,
Nothing is impossible
With God by our side.

Learning from experience
We must do our best,
The Saviour will guide us,
He will bring such happiness.

Challenges will rise
And hopes will succeed,
The seasons of life keep changing
As we age so gracefully.

LEAD ME IN YOUR FOOTSTEPS

Lead me in your footsteps
When the way I cannot see,
The road is dim ahead
But Your light shines on me.

Lead me in Your footsteps
Shrouded in Your peace and love,
Teach me Your ways
As You guide me from above.

Lead me in Your footsteps
To charge me with love divine,
To drink from Your cup
The fruit of the vine.

Lead me in Your footsteps,
A print of humility,
Always upon my heart,
The risen Christ for me.

CLAIM A HAPPY DAY

When I start my daily chores,
My mood depicts my day,
But if I meet You Lord
Your Spirit leads the way.

I may feel a little low,
It's then I reach for you,
I simply say "come to me",
That's all I have to do.

I ask You Lord to cheer me up
And give me a happy heart,
To get me through my day,
While the hours pass.

I lift my thoughts to Heaven's loft,
A lighter step I claim,
Thank You for Your Spirit Lord
Who takes my blues away.

PART TWO

"I have the strength to face all
conditions by the power that Christ gives me."

Philippians 4 : 13

BE ASSURED...
BY THE POWER OF HIS NAME...

"The Lord himself will lead you and be with you. He will not fail you or abandon you..."

Deuteronomy 31 : 8

A THREAD OF BELONGING

Lord, in Your peace and calm
I ponder my life,
A thread of belonging
Is what I find.

In those moments
I confess the truth,
My thread of belonging
Leads to You.

Your tender love
Beckons me on,
Though trials approach me
You keep me strong.

A thread of belonging,
Strengthened by Your grace
That you give abundantly
To all who seek Your face.

Yes, a thread of faith
Will swell like a river,
Flowing in Your pure love
That will always last forever.

IN PERFECT COMMUNION

In perfect communion
With the Holy One,
When there are no distractions
Two become one.

In perfect communion
My thoughts fly to a higher place
Where my Saviour never leaves me,
He walks my daily pace.

In perfect communion
He is by my side,
Acceptance comes full circle
With a love to last all time.

In perfect communion
My trust comes to the test,
Sweetness flows between us,
I lay my ahead upon His breast.

SILENT LISTENER, UNSEEN GUEST

He is the Lord Almighty
Who came to serve,
Forever the silent listener
To our every word.

He is the unseen guest
At every gathering,
Large or small He is there
Without us even knowing!

Just because we can't see Him,
Doesn't mean He isn't there,
Our actions would be so different
And our hearts would truly care.

The world would be a better place,
I'm sure we would be our best
When He appears in His great majesty,
The silent listener, unseen guest.

YOUR HEART CAN BE HIS HOME

Your heart can be His home
When you surrender to Him,
Allow His Holy Spirit
To reside within.

You will know pure love
As you commune with Him,
Every day is an open page
When you submit to Him.

We don't know today
What the dawn will bring,
But open your heart to His Spirit,
He will supply your everything.

So summon the Lord of Lords
To your open heart,
Make it His home
To enrich your daily path.

THE TEST OF TIME

I commit the day to You Lord
To bring Your love to the surface,
To show Your works
As I live in Your service.

To use Your gifts
By having a listening ear,
To show Your love
That is so dear.

To demonstrate kindness
That overflows,
Is one of Your gifts
That Your love will show.

You stand for unity,
For Your love to abide,
As we walk with You
We'll stand the test of time.

THE NEXT TWENTY FOUR HOURS

Thank you Dear One
For every sunrise,
No matter what it brings,
You are by my side.

My focus is on You
To get me through the day,
Keep my emotions calm,
That is what I pray.

Through the next twenty four hours,
I need your guiding hand
To help me make decisions
To do the best I can.

So thank you Dear One
As Your will comes to pass,
Help me through each day
Is all that I ask.

IN YOUR HEART OF HEARTS…
SEEK HIM…

"…know that I am God…"

Psalm 46 : 10

THE HUMAN HEART

The human heart houses emotion
In many different ways,
It rages battles to survive
But peace is what we crave.

The human heart weeps with sorrow
So deep we may never be the same,
Lord have mercy upon us
So we can turn from the hurt and pain.

The human heart reflects our behaviour
With words that can swoop or soar,
But when we know Jesus,
His love will teach us more.

The human heart can rejoice
In moments so divine,
We can choose to have a happy heart,
If we will only make up our minds.

SHARE TODAY

Life will bring its challenges,
Some big, some small,
But walking with the Saviour,
He will help you through them all.

Ask Him for strength and peace,
Claim His help always,
Be sure He will hear you,
He will share your task today.

No challenge is too great for Him,
He's longing for your request,
To help you through today
So you can do your best.

His answer will arrive
From lips that called the first day,
He's waiting for your request,
So share with Him today.

OUR WATCHFUL SHEPHERD

We are the Saviour's sheep,
So precious in His sight,
Follow Him we must
All through our life.

He speaks to His flock
But sometimes we miss His call,
Swept up in daily life
We can stumble and fall.

Some days we wander off
On a different track,
But our watchful Shepherd
Will always bring us back.

We have our place in His fold
Where His loving eye keeps watch
Over His lambs forever,
His care will never stop.

STEP OUT IN HIS LIGHT

Walking in His light
Is the best we can do,
With every little care
He wants to help us through.

On those cloudy days
No sunshine to be seen,
Don't stay in the shadows,
Step into His light to be free.

The future seems to be lost,
No horizon in sight,
The Master will steer your course,
Step out in His light.

Hope will rise in you,
Though a challenge you may see,
Talk to the Saviour
You can rise to victory!

SOLID GROUND

Stand on solid ground,
The only place to be,
In faith we have Jesus
He will bring security.

He is the living Christ
For every person in this world,
To accept Him as their Saviour,
Their cares can be unfurled.

No more inhibitions
To store up inside,
Stand on solid ground,
Keep your faith; just try.

Confess to the Saviour,
Claim Him King of Kings,
You'll stand on solid ground
And secure peace within.

ONE TO ONE

One to one Lord,
That's You and me,
My shining light
You are to me.

Your Spirit watches over
As my daily life unfolds,
You send Your love divine
As I take Your hand to hold.

I close my eyes in reverence
To bring You closer still,
As You send Your love divine
To fulfill Your holy will.

So thank you Dear Lord
As we nestle one to one,
My Master and my Saviour,
One day we will be one.

TALK TO HIM...
HE'S YOUR COUNSELLOR...

"...My grace is all you need, for my power is strongest when you are weak..."

2 Corinthians 12 : 9

YOUR HOPE HE WILL RESTORE

Talk to the Saviour anytime
When your heart feels bruised or sore,
Your peace and calm is shattered
But your hope He will restore.

He's always your friend,
The greatest counsellor of all,
Your wounds He will soothe
When His name you call.

You can ask for Jesus,
He will carry you through,
His Spirit will deliver,
That's His promise to you.

Eternal life is yours indeed,
Repent to the Saviour on bended knee,
Your hope He will restore,
He's all you'll ever need.

MY POEMS

My poems are my thoughts Lord
In praise I bow to You,
As I write these words of love,
For Your lambs to follow You.

My poems are my thoughts
To come before Your Throne,
With all I have to bring,
It's my soul that you own.

My poems are my thoughts
To worship You alone,
Anoint me Lord forever
To help Your beloved home.

My poems are my prayers
For everyone to read,
I pray they will bring us all
Closer to Thee.

MY MIND'S EYE

My friend from eternity,
From You I cannot hide,
I have a picture of You
In my mind's eye.

It brings me calm to see You there,
I don't feel alone,
My thoughts are hushed for a while,
In me You've made Your home.

I can take You anywhere
You never leave my side,
When I'm happy or sad You're with me,
In my mind's eye.

Help me not to rush
But to remember You are there
In my mind's eye,
Your wondrous face so fair!

FORGET REGRET

Forget regret,
There's no going back,
Replace it in your heart
With His love that never lacks.

Just for that moment
If a choice wasn't sound,
Regret takes its toll,
Look to sacred ground.

The Saviour took regret
On the road to Calvary,
He nailed it to His Cross
So forever we are free.

The Saviour wants us to be happy,
Only in Him can this be,
Forget regret today,
He will set you free.

Look to Him for healing,
Love Him endlessly,
Forget regret forever,
He forgave you at Calvary.

MY HEART YOU OWN

I bring to Your Altar Lord
Upon Your heavenly Throne,
My prayers whispered quietly
Because my heart You own.

In full surrender
I tell You my all,
My deepest desires
And plans I recall.

With my heart wide open
I bow at Your feet,
Believing in faith
My cares You will meet.

Teach my heart faithfulness
As I come to You in prayer,
Guide me along quietly,
You are always there.

THE BEST IS YET TO COME

When your world seems dim
And you feel all alone,
Turn to the Saviour
Upon His Throne.

All is not lost,
We have the "Light of the World"
Though life seems barren,
All is well.

He will never leave you,
He is by your side,
He will carry your weary heart,
While you wait for the turning tide.

Nothing stays the same forever,
Trust in His great love,
The future will unfold,
The best is yet to come.

The best is yet to come
If we sustain our love and more,
Use our trust and faith,
He will come with His rewards.

TEACH ME LORD…

…and so be completely filled with
the very nature of God."

Ephesians 3 : 19

MAKE HIM YOUR GOAL

Make Jesus your goal
In everything you do,
Look to the Master,
His love is ever-true.

Make Him your goal
Every day of your life,
With Him by your side
Everything will come right.

Aim for the best
In life every day,
You will be rewarded
In every way.

Make Him your goal,
Receive His wondrous gifts,
A happier life you'll know
If you'll only turn to Him.

MAKE A FRESH START

Everyone needs Jesus
For a peaceful heart,
Turn from the hardships of life,
Make a fresh start.

He can help you beat
Those wild and testing days,
Try to look for the positives
In His golden rays.

Replace the negative to positive
And change the sour to sweet,
Then rise from low to high
When you bow at His mercy seat.

Make your mind up
To have a happy heart,
Ask Jesus to help you
You can make a fresh start.

KEEP ME ON TRACK

All my wants may not surface
In this life of mine,
But accepting the Lord's will
They will show in His good time.

It's taken many years
For my acceptance to take shape
Of His will completely,
In my life to overtake.

His plan will reign supreme
No matter what I do,
In time it will come to pass,
I just have to see it through.

But in loving Him He gives me
The patience that I lack,
To see His will in time
To keep me on track.

HEAL ME LORD

Thank You for healing me Lord
When my heart is ready to forgive,
Your lessons in life aren't easy,
But in Your ways I must live.

I pray for Your anointing
To give me a thankful heart,
To be willing to obey
Your will that You impart.

You solve all my problems
When in faith I trust in You,
In willingness I wait,
That's all I have to do.

My wait may be a long time
But to gain I must lose,
Changing life situations,
But it's You who I choose.

So direct my footsteps
All my life through,
I pray for Your healing Lord,
I want to praise and worship You.

IN HIS SHADOW

I'm in His shadow,
I'm committing the day
To His holy plan,
For me the only way.

I'm in His shadow
As He guides me through the day,
With eager faith I follow Him
For He's prepared my way.

I feel safe in His shadow,
I can't lose my way,
I'm in His shadow
Come sunshine or rain.

I'm in His shadow
What joy floods within,
My Saviour, my Master,
I will always follow Him.

AN OPEN HEART

An open heart lies waiting
With a load too heavy to bear,
A pierced hand is reaching
To fill it with a love so rare.

An open heart so delicate
Has wounds from life itself,
These can only be healed
With the Saviour's help.

Nothing on earth can match
The Saviour's eternal love,
Open your heart to Jesus,
God's own precious Son.

He will fill your open heart
With His joy divine,
He will calm and soothe your worries
And bring peace to your mind.

Eternal life can be yours
When you confess to the risen Christ,
"Forgive me for my sin,
In You I receive eternal life".

HE'S BY YOUR SIDE

He's the friend you can talk to
He's by your side,
In need or praise you can say,
"Lord be mine".

He wants you to call for Him
Every day of your life,
To help you through the hours
Say, "Lord be mine".

There's no other way
To find inner strength,
Talk to the Saviour
Your help in need.

In trust and faith you will succeed,
The Saviour is by your side,
Strength will be revealed
In His perfect time!

GIFTS HE LONGS TO GIVE

Present your desires
To the King of Kings,
Ask for all your needs,
Take His hand to succeed.

In Him your heart will shine
With gifts He longs to give,
Compassion, truth and grace
Are truly on His list.

Those quiet chats He loves
When you whisper some words,
Your happy days will prosper,
It's you He longs to serve.

DIRECTION

North, South, East or West
Which way do I go?
I believe a door will open
From Jesus I know.

In life we come to crossroads,
Decisions we have to make,
May your heart always be
In the right place.

I pray the way will be shady
With streams and grassy fields,
No steep hills to climb
But a harvest of perfect yield.

You may have obstacles to pass
But the Saviour is ready to act,
He's your heavenly guide
To keep you on track.

COMMIT THE DAY

Commit each day to the Lord
As forward you go,
Walking in His shadow
What a joy you will know.

He will change your heart
To suit the day,
Even though His steps
May take you a different way.

Just in a whisper
He can remove
Resentment and frustration
If you ask Him to.

Commit each day to the Lord
You need Him by your side,
As each day rolls along
Ask Him to be your guide.

LIFE'S QUALITIES

Endurance, truth and wisdom
We need from the Lord,
These choices we make
We can take from His store.

Patience, peace and calm
We need every day,
Pray for these qualities
To help you on your way.

When searching for life's qualities
His Book can be your guide,
His Word will show you how
Because you're precious in His sight.

When we have the Saviour
Living in our heart,
These qualities will abide in us
To remind us who we are.

As children of God
Life's qualities will remain,
His great love will prevail,
He will never change.

YOUR NEEDS WILL BE MET

Walking with the Saviour
On your daily path,
He's willing and waiting
And knows what you will ask.

He wants you to share
The contents of your heart,
Don't hesitate to talk to Him,
You only have to ask.

Share your joys and cares
With the Holy One,
How wonderful to talk
To God's only Son.

It's then you come together
In His majesty and grace,
Your needs will be met
In His time and place.

PART THREE

"For it is by God's grace that you have been saved through faith...."

Ephesians 2 : 8

GATHER ME UNDER YOUR WINGS...

"How precious, O God, is your constant love!
We find protection under the shadow of your wings."

Psalm 36 : 7

THE VOICE IN ME

Lord, I've found a voice in me
In many different ways,
It's Your Spirit I hear
As He lives in me each day.

I feel so blessed
To be prompted this way,
When I listen to His voice
My fears just run away.

He lays on my heart
A conscious thought,
Then brings someone to mind
Who needs the prayer You taught.

His baptism of love
That flows over me,
Brings Your power and grace
That leads me to "believe".

He shows me Your ways
In great magnitude,
I love Him so dearly,
Holy Spirit sent by You!

YOU TURNED MY LIFE AROUND

You've turned my life around Lord
Since I surrendered to You,
My journey passed through challenges
But I still look to You.

Over hills and into valleys
You are always there,
My counsellor always
My everything I share.

My favourite times are the mountain tops,
I can see Heaven's distant shore,
The jewels that lie sparkling
Are the gifts of Your rewards.

You've turned my life around Lord
Since I've truly listened to You,
Commitment and desire I crave
To meet You when I'm through.

TODAY WE HAVE JESUS

Yesterday is gone with the sunset,
Tomorrow waits for the dawn,
The future lies in His hands
Waiting to be born.

We can't change what happened yesterday
If regret is the call,
But today we have Jesus
Who will catch us when we fall.

We can learn from yesterday
With hope in our heart,
Because today with the Saviour
We can make a fresh start.

Yes today we have Jesus
As the sun rises high,
He's waiting to help you
As the hours pass you by.

PRIVILEGED POWERS

Loved ones left behind
With the promise "we'll meet again",
Carry on through life,
Do the best they can.

In dreams they come to me,
I am with them once again,
How real it surely seems,
Their love they freely send.

No boundaries bind them down,
They're as free as a bird,
Heaven's privileged powers
On earth are still unheard.

In His presence they'll always live,
Their love forever blends,
As they praise and worship Jesus
In His kingdom without end.

PURE GOLD

Pure gold, my Saviour
Perfect in every way,
Creator of the universe
Who takes my sin away.

Pure gold, Christ Jesus,
The Holy Father's Son,
Divine eternal Lord
Who is pure love.

Pure gold, my Master
Taught me the Lord's Prayer,
To worship Him alone,
I am in His care.

Pure gold, my King of Kings,
Brighter than the sun,
He is the Light of the world,
One day we will be one.

RUNAWAY TEARS

Runaway tears flow anytime
And strike on any cord,
Emotion from your soul
Into your heart they will fall.

Runaway tears overflow
From eyes full of pain,
Through sorrow deep inside,
They fall like gentle rain.

Runaway tears can flow from joy,
A surprise that's come to light,
Indeed a special blessing
That makes your day so bright.

Runaway tears whether happy or sad
Is emotion running free,
The Saviour knows each tear drop
He says "beloved, come to me".

LITTLE BY LITTLE...
FAITH WILL GROW...

"So then, faith comes from hearing the message, and the message comes through preaching Christ."

Romans 10 : 17

SWEET VICTORY

My King, my Lord, my Friend,
The narrow road is sweet but high,
Some days as I journey
I have to check my thoughts inside.

To keep them high above
When bells ring loud and clear,
To advance to the front
And steer away from fear.

There are many obstacles
To negotiate along,
Highs and lows I meet
But my Lord, He makes me strong.

Then I will know sweet victory
As I cross the finish line,
Meeting Him in paradise
Sweet victory will be mine.

WHERE AM I

Where am I Lord
In the scheme of things?
I have to keep my faith
And see what it brings.

Where am I Lord?
As I seek Your plan,
Guide me through
With Your pierced hand.

Shield me, protect me
When confusion reigns,
Along life's road
Help me see a clearer way.

So help me Lord to see
Your plan for me,
Guide me all the way
To where You want me.

ETERNAL SPRING

Drink from His eternal spring,
Receive His gifts for life,
Your joy will overflow
From He who makes things right.

He desires your commitment
For truth, love and grace,
These gifts He freely gives
To those who've seen His face.

His eternal spring will flow
Of gifts He longs to give,
Wisdom, strength and peace
When He lives within.

So drink from His eternal spring
To live forever more,
Accept His gift of love
When He knocks on your heart's door.

OVERFLOWING HOLINESS

In overflowing holiness
You will want to make a stand,
Freshly born again
When you take the Saviour's hand.

In faith you come to Him
And carry a humble heart,
Overflowing holiness
Will come to light your path.

The change will be heartfelt,
Conscious thoughts of cleansing and grace
Come to bless your life
When you see His holy face.

Anything is possible,
Your faith will reveal,
Knowing the humble Christ,
Your heart He will surely steal.

WALK IN UNISON WITH CHRIST

Walk in unison with Christ,
Step by step as you go,
Sometimes your life is busy,
He is still there you know.

There are so many needs
In the world today,
The Lord uses His helpers
To show His ways.

To walk in unison with Christ
With compassion, trust and grace,
And show a little mercy
Will indeed feed your faith.

He will ignite the Spirit's flame
Of eternal love,
When you walk in unison with Christ,
Many blessings will come.

PRECIOUS GIFTS

His precious gifts of love,
Life, peace and calm,
Wisdom, strength and truth
All anointed in His balm.

Ours for the taking,
How precious they are,
So rich we can be,
From His hand beyond the stars.

These precious gifts are yours
From His Cross at Calvary,
Take and enjoy
From the one who set you free.

No one else can give
These precious gifts from "Thee",
Only the Lord Jesus Christ
Can prepare you for Eternity.

PART FOUR

"Then Pilate handed Jesus over to them to be crucified. So they took charge of Jesus. He went out, carrying his cross…"

John 19 : 16, 17

A PRICE...
WE CAN NEVER PAY...

"...above him were written these words:
"This is the King of the Jews."

Luke 23 : 38

FOLLOW YOUR HEART TO THE CROSS

Follow your heart to the Cross,
A place of surrender,
Lay your heart open wide
To Christ Jesus our Redeemer.

Follow your heart to the Cross
Where thoughts and desires cease,
Your world seems to stop,
In need, you bow at its feet.

Follow your heart to the Cross,
A place of sacrifice and truth,
Where the precious Lord Jesus
Gave His life for me and you.

Follow your heart to the Cross,
You will stand on sacred ground,
Your feelings and emotions released,
Where God's Eternity is found.

The Saviour Himself will meet you there
As you confess your forgiven sin,
He paid the price once only
So you can spend Eternity with Him.

YOUR GREATEST BLESSING IN A VOW

Your eternal love and grace is ours,
Your greatest blessing in a vow
You made to Your Father above,
When You took Calvary's cup,

Your greatest blessing saves the world
For everyone who hears "the Word",
Give your heart to the living Christ,
You will receive eternal life.

Your greatest blessing in a vow
Was the Cross You took for me,
My sin You paid at Calvary
Now You have set me free.

Soothe me, heal me, comfort me,
Charge me Lord with Thee,
Cleanse me in Your love right now,
Your greatest blessing in a vow.

GOD'S HOLY PLAN

Two millenniums ago
God's Holy plan came forth,
A Saviour, His Son
Humbly and quietly was born.

God's Holy plan revealed
In the Scriptures long ago,
The Messiah would be born
Because He loves us so.

He grew into a man
Then began His ministry,
That would take Him to a Cross
Where He died for you and me.

He paid for our sin
So we could be free,
An example of pure love
Shown to the world at Calvary.

God raised Him to life
From the tomb, in victory
He lives for us in heaven,
God's Holy plan came to be.

THE HOLY...
AND THE DIVINE...

"After the Lord Jesus had talked with them, he was taken up to heaven and sat at the right side of God."

Mark 16 : 19

A BRAND NEW LOVE

A brand new love is waiting
To touch a lonely heart,
It comes from Eternity
With grace, peace and calm.

This brand new love so mighty
Comes with a Holy Crown,
Held in pierced hands
That together, once were bound.

This brand new love
Is just a breath away
Whisper "Saviour come,
Change me now today".

With your brand new love
You will never be alone,
Forever you are His
When you bow before His Throne.

FOLLOW HIS PATH

Follow His path in the light
Where you can never get lost,
He is the Saviour of the world
Who paid Calvary's cost.

Follow His path all your days
Though cross roads you will meet,
You will make the right decision
If His Will you seek.

Follow His path all your days
Though emotions take their toll,
Pray for His healing and mercy,
Your worries He will solve.

Follow His path all your days,
Come sunshine or rain,
His wings will give you shelter,
In His love you will be saved.

HUMBLY AND QUIETLY…
THE SAVIOUR WAS BORN…

"…on their way they saw the same star they had seen in the East. When they saw it, how happy they were, what joy was theirs! It went ahead of them until it stopped over the place where the child was."

Matthew 2 : 9 - 10

A JOURNEY LIKE NO OTHER

A journey like no other
Was made over hills and plains.
Through cold winter nights
Joseph and Mary made their way.

Bethlehem was the destination
For the Census to be held,
So they journeyed afar
For the count of themselves.

Mary heavy with child,
They searched for a room that night,
The Inn only offered a stable
But the Star of the East shone bright!

Mary safely delivered the Saviour,
The Wise Men came with gifts for Him,
This journey like no other
Brought forth the precious King of Kings!

A GIFT BEYOND COMPARE

A gift beyond compare
Delivered one Holy Night,
Heavenly voices rang out
To tell of this Holy sight.

The glory of angels shone down
On shepherds in the fields,
With news, "the Messiah is coming
In a Manger" was revealed!

A blazing star lit up
A stable in Bethlehem,
To guide eastern travellers
Known as the "Three Wise Men".

In wonder and awe they fell
Upon their knees to behold
The Messiah; King of Kings,
With gifts of Frankincense, Myrrh and Gold!

A gift beyond compare
From God Himself,
The Christ Child in the Manger,
The Chosen Saviour of the World!

UNSPOKEN LOVE

Mary and Joseph travelled to Bethlehem
For the Census of the land
Where she would deliver the child,
All part of God's Holy plan.

God chose her to raise His child
Who would be her very first,
The awe of that Holy Night
When Mary gave birth.

God's power and glory shone bright
Upon the stable filled with awe,
And the unspoken love poured out
From the Christ; the Holy Newborn!

The Magi came forth with gifts,
With the cattle and sheep who adored
The tiny Saviour in the Manger,
God's Son will live forever more!

FAITHFUL SERVANTS

Faithful servants; Mary and Joseph,
Who loved God and obeyed His command
To bring into the world His Son
And lovingly raised Him to be a man.

Mary held in her heart
The awe of that Holy Night,
How the Star revealed the stable;
A place of glory and light.

The gifts given by the Wise Men
So profound in many ways,
They carried along with them
To a home where they would be safe.

They were faithful servants of the Master,
Right up to His final days,
Bethlehem will always be
A sacred place that brought the Holy Babe!

ALSO BY CLAIRE GROSE

ABOUT THE AUTHOR

Claire worked as a Government Public Servant in the Lands Department, Adelaide, South Australia until she married and became a mother of two boys.

She later returned to the work force during which time she gained a "Living Hope" Phone Counselling certificate which influenced her need to help others.

Through this and personal experience she found herself inspired by God's love to put pen to paper.

PHOTO CREDITS

COVER PHOTO: The banks of the River Clyde, Lanark, (Castlebank) Scotland – taken by Hugh Kennedy

Page 2: Roses, Veale Gardens; Adelaide - S.A. – Claire Grose
Page 12: Single Rose; Elizabeth Downs, S.A.– Claire Grose
Page 24: Garden Scene; Lyndoch, S.A. – Claire Grose
Page 31: Lavender Bush; Mallala, S.A. – Lynne & Eileen
Page 39: Rock Garden Setting; Lyndoch, S.A. – Claire Grose
Page 47: Potted Fern; Tanunda, S.A. - Val
Page 55: Duck Family; Fremont Park, S.A. – Claire Grose
Page 70: Sand Dunes; Semaphore Beach, S.A. – Claire Grose
Page 78: Pond view; Fremont Park, S.A. – Claire Grose
Page 87: Red Poppies; Mallala, S.A. - Lynne & Eileen
Page 92: Sunset; Largs Bay, S.A. – Claire Grose
Page 96: Hay Bales; Bethany, S.A. – Claire Grose

A THREAD OF BELONGING

www.ingramcontent.com/pod-product-compliance
Lightning Source LLC
Chambersburg PA
CBHW051539010526
44107CB00064B/2783